Wraps Around the World

Wraps Around the World

FUSION FAST FOOD

By Iris Sutton and Shelby Sewell

Photography by Marsha Burns

Abbeville Press   Publishers

New York London Paris

Designed by Ed Marquand with assistance by Melanie Milkie
Edited by Meredith Wolf Schizer and Marie Weiler
Illustration on page 14 by Craig Orback
Produced by Marquand Books, Inc., Seattle.
Marquand Books wishes to thank Manine Rosa Golden for
her initial research on this project.

First edition
10 9 8 7 6 5 4 3 2 1

Library of Congress Cataloging-in-Publication Data
Sutton, Iris.
    Wraps around the world / by Iris Sutton and Shelby
Sewell : photography by Marsha Burns. — 1st ed.
        p.   cm.
    Includes index.
    ISBN 0-7892-0351-0
    1. Stuffed foods (Cookery) 2. Cookery, International.
I. Sewell, Shelby. II. Title.
TX836.S88   1998
641.8—dc21   97-49589

Front jacket/cover: Lentil and Sultana Salad, recipe on page 50
Back jacket/cover: Lobster Salad, recipe on page 55
Half title page: Smoked Salmon Roulade, recipe on page 41
Frontispiece: Scrambled Eggs and Black Beans with Red Pepper
Sauce, recipe on page 26
Page 4: Greek Salad with Hummus, recipe on page 49

Please note: All recipes in *Wraps Around the World* have been
tested to be safe. However, always consult with your physician
if you have any doubts or if you have a medical condition or
any allergies. Author and publisher accept no liability with
regard to the use of recipes contained in this book.

Contents

What do curried vegetables, barbecued pork, and chicken salad have in common? As filling for tortillas, pita bread, phyllo pastry, or egg roll wrappers they make terrific handheld meals that are portable and delicious. Meet the wrap, the imaginative and healthy food that's sweeping the nation. A combination burrito, sandwich, and hot meal, a wrap can be filled with just about anything for a satisfying breakfast, lunch, or dinner, or even an hors d'oeuvre or dessert.

The wrap is not a recent invention. It has its roots in the cuisines of many different cultures around the world: Mexican burritos and tacos, French crepes, Vietnamese spring rolls, Chinese egg rolls, and Middle Eastern falafel. The recipes in this book were inspired by these diverse cooking traditions and use a variety of international ingredients and flavors.

The recipes make liberal use of vegetables and are generally low in fat, so you can enjoy a flavorful, imaginative meal that is also healthy and satisfying. This book is a must for people of all ages who are nutritionally aware and interested in international foods, whether you want a gourmet meal or one that is quick and easy to prepare. They make the perfect meal to nibble as you go, go, go.

Brown Rice, Tofu, and Vegetables,
recipe on page 52

Be sure to experiment with the Wrap Mode section of this book. Once you've followed some of these recipes, you'll be eager to put together your own combinations. Roll up your favorite vegetable stir-fry in a rice-paper wrapper or your dinner leftovers in a tortilla. You'll wonder why you've been grabbing a slice of pizza at lunch, when you could have been bringing Thai vegetables and peanut sauce in a wrap from home. Why buy a muffin when you could have wrapped *huevos rancheros* for breakfast? All you need to know to make imaginative, healthy meals is stuffed into *Wraps Around the World.*

Sweet Peppers and Black Beans with
Arugula, Mango, and Avocado Salad,
recipe on page 46

1. Mound the filling in the middle of the round.

2. Fold in the sides over the filling.

The Wrappers

Any flat bread or pastry makes an excellent wrapper. Those used in the recipes in this book are described on the following pages. You can also experiment with greens, like radicchio (see page 55), or meats, such as prosciutto (see page 31), or even flank steak (see page 77).

The basic roll

Most of the round breads will use the same basic roll. For any of these, before you add the filling, warm the bread in the oven for just a few seconds to make it pliable. Or, if you're preparing more than just one or two wraps, place the bread on plates, mound the filling, and then place in the microwave or a warm oven for just a few seconds. This sequence will keep the tortillas from cooling and becoming brittle before you have a chance to roll them.

3. Fold the end nearest you over the filling.

4. Roll up, being careful to keep the sides tucked in.

5. Place on a plate, seam side down.

Crepes

Crepes are the one wrapper you'll want to make yourself. They're quick and easy and almost melt in your mouth when they're fresh. Follow the recipe on page 24.

To roll: Mound filling on the half of the crepe nearest you. Fold the crepe over the filling and simply roll up.

Recipes using crepes are on pages 24 and 82.

Egg roll wrappers

Egg roll wrappers are available in the refrigerated ethnic foods section of the supermarket or in Asian specialty food stores. Aso called spring roll wrappers or lumpia, they come in 8-inch (20-cm) rounds, about 25 to a package.

Recipe using egg roll wrappers is on page 38.

To fold egg roll wrappers:

1. Place the wrapper with one corner facing you. Mound the filling on the half of the wrapper nearest you.

2. Fold the near corner over the filling and tuck in the sides.

3. Roll up.

4. Brush the end with egg wash (see Note, page 38) to seal.

Lavash

Lavash, also called "soft cracker bread," can be found in the freezer section of the supermarket. It comes in 14-inch (35.5-cm) rounds, three pieces per package. You can also sometimes find it dry, in which case you should moisten it according to package instructions before use.

To roll: Follow the basic roll.

Recipes using lavash are on pages 57 and 75.

Naan bread

Naan bread is available in the frozen foods section of the supermarket. It comes in 6-inch (15.25-cm) rounds, six per package, and simply needs to be warmed before use. It is also available ready to eat in Middle Eastern specialty food stores.

To roll: Follow the basic roll.

Recipes using naan bread are on pages 50 and 61.

Phyllo pastry

Phyllo, or fillo, pastry is available in the frozen foods section of the supermarket. The paper-thin sheets are about 14 inches (35.5 cm) square. Before using, defrost in the refrigerator for a few hours or overnight. Remove the thawed dough from the package and gently unroll it. Carefully separate one sheet from the stack and lay it on a clean, dry work surface. Brush the sheet lightly with melted butter and lay another sheet on top of it. Brush the second sheet with butter. Proceed in this manner until you have the required number of sheets. Use immediately. While working, keep the unused dough covered with a damp cloth, as the dough will dry out quickly. Unused sheets of pastry can be rerolled and refrigerated or refrozen.

Phyllo is very fragile, but don't let it intimidate you! Organize your workspace so you have only the materials you need, placed where you can use them efficiently. Then work cooly and patiently.

To fold: Follow the instructions for your particular recipe.

Recipes using phyllo pastry are on pages 43 and 71.

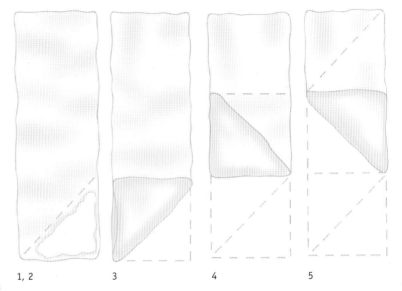

1, 2   3   4   5

To do the flag fold specified on page 71:

1. Lay the strips lengthwise in front of you.

2. Mound filling in the right corner.

3. Fold right corner over, even with left side of strip.

4. Fold the tip up.

5. Now fold to the right, now up, now to the left.

Pita bread

Pita bread is available in the bread or deli section of any supermarket. Place a single pita pocket on a clean, dry work surface and carefully slice off the top edge of the round or slice in half, as the recipe or your whim dictates. Refrigerate after opening the package.

Recipes using pita bread are on pages 20, 49, 52, 68, and 72.

Pizza dough

Pizza dough is available in the frozen foods section of the supermarket, either in 1-pound (454-g) white or whole-wheat balls that must be thawed and rolled out or in 14-inch (35.5-cm) rounds. The rolled-out variety comes 8 pieces to a 4½-pound (126-g) package.

To roll: Mound filling on the half nearest you. Fold the dough over the filling and simply roll up.

Recipes using pizza dough are on pages 51 and 65.

Puff pastry

Puff pastry can be found in the frozen foods section of the supermarket. A 14-ounce (392-g) package holds one sheet of pastry.

To fold: Mound pastry on one half of the small rounds you have cut, as specified in your particular recipe. Fold in half and crimp the edge. Brush with beaten egg to seal.

Recipes using puff pastry are on pages 42 and 44.

Rice paper *(bánh tráng)*

Rice paper is available at Asian markets and in the Asian foods section of some supermarkets. It comes in 6- and 8-inch (15.25- and 20-cm) rounds and 8-inch (20-cm) squares, and may also be called spring roll wrappers. To use, place one or two sheets of rice paper in a large bowl of lukewarm water. Soak until soft, one to two minutes. Be careful not to soak too long or the rice paper will disintegrate. Drain softened rice papers on a cotton or linen towel before using. Store unsoaked rice papers in a cool, dry place.

To roll: If using round papers, follow the basic roll. If using square papers, follow the instructions for egg roll wrappers.

Recipes using rice paper are on pages 34 and 79.

Tortillas

Standard flour and corn tortillas are available in the dairy section of any supermarket. You can find whole-wheat and flavored tortillas, for example, tomato, pesto, or spinach, in the deli section of the supermarket and at specialty food stores. Before using, warm tortillas in the oven for just a few seconds to make them pliable. Refrigerate package after opening.

To roll: Follow the basic roll.

Recipes using tortillas are on pages 19, 21, 22, 26, 28, 46, 59, 60, 66, and 67.

Wonton wrappers

Wonton wrappers are available in the refrigerated ethnic foods section of the supermarket or in Asian specialty stores. Wonton wrappers are 3½ inches (9 cm) square and come about 40 to a package. You can also use *gyoza* wrappers, which are the same as wonton wrappers except 3½ inches (9 cm) round.

To fold wonton wrappers:

1. Mound filling on the lower half of each wrapper, and with a brush, moisten the edges with water.

2. Fold the wrapper in half over the filling to form a triangle and pinch to thoroughly seal the edges.

3. Fold the two side points over the filled middle and moisten the points with water.

4. Pinch the points to seal.

Getting into Wrap Mode

Making wraps can be as quick and easy as opening your cupboard or refrigerator and pulling out whatever you find. Rice and small pastas —like couscous and orzo—make good fillers to pair up with chopped vegetables—sweet peppers and red onion are especially flavorful—and beans—try black beans or garbanzos. Moisten the filling with tahini sauce, salsa, or even your favorite salad dressing to spice up the filling and keep it from getting too dry. Keep large tortillas on hand so you're always prepared to wrap up your tasty creations.

The next five recipes should give you ideas for creating your own wraps from foods you have in the cupboard or leftovers from last night's dinner. Or, if you're ready to try something a little more formal that requires a bit more preparation, go ahead to the following sections.

Remember, in these and all the recipes in this book: *Don't be afraid to substitute!* Like the bread they're wrapped in, these recipes are flexible and are meant to be tailored to suit your lifestyle.

Barbecued Pork with Rice and Beans

This is an excellent use for leftovers after a summer barbecue. Substitute chicken or steak for the pork if that's what you have on hand.

½ cup (120 ml) barbecue sauce
1 pork tenderloin (about 8 ounces; 228 g), cooked and shredded
½ cup (90 g) baked beans
4 flour tortillas
½ cup (100 g) rice, cooked according to package instructions
1 cup (4 ounces; 112 g) grated cheddar cheese
1 bunch mustard greens, washed and dried

- Preheat the oven to 350°F (175°C).

- In a small saucepan, combine the barbecue sauce and the pork and warm through. Warm the beans in the oven or microwave.

- Heat the tortillas for a few seconds so they are pliable, then place them on a clean, dry work surface. Put some of the beans and the rice on each. Cover with the barbecued pork, the cheddar, and a few leaves of the mustard greens. Roll up, put on a baking sheet, and place in the oven until the cheese melts.

Serves 4

Steak and Potatoes with Puttanesca Sauce

You can easily substitute the flank steak in this recipe with sautéed ground beef or poached and shredded chicken.

Sauce:

½ cup (120 ml) extra-virgin olive oil

1 can (2 ounces; 56 g) anchovy fillets, undrained

4 cloves garlic, crushed

1 can (28 ounces; 794 g) plum tomatoes, drained

1 jar (2½ ounces; 88 ml) capers, drained

1½ cups (180 g) Meditteranean-style black olives, pitted and coarsely chopped

freshly ground pepper

4 pita pockets

½ pound (228 g) flank steak, broiled or grilled to medium rare and thinly sliced

1 cup mashed potatoes

- *Make the sauce:* Place the oil, anchovies, and garlic in a heavy saucepan. Mash thoroughly to form a paste. Add the tomatoes, capers, and olives. Stir over medium heat until just bubbling. Reduce the heat to low and simmer, uncovered, for 1 hour, stirring occasionally. Season with pepper.

- Cut each of the pita pockets in half and fill with the steak and mashed potatoes. Top with a generous spoonful of the sauce and serve. Freeze any leftover sauce to use on pasta at a later date. In fact, it's a good idea to make a double batch just to have on hand.

Serves 4

Thai-style

This Asian treat is a snap to wrap up!

4 flour tortillas
½ cup (120 ml) peanut sauce (see Note)
⅓ cup (65 g) rice, cooked according to package
    instructions
½ large chicken breast, poached, cooled, and shredded
2 cups (112 g) bean sprouts
chili-garlic sauce (see Note)

- Heat the tortillas for a few seconds so they are pliable, then lay them out on a clean, dry work surface.

- With a spatula, spread peanut sauce on each tortilla. Add the rice, chicken, and sprouts and drizzle lightly with the chili-garlic sauce. Roll up and serve.

Note: Peanut sauce can be found in the deli or meat section of your supermarket. Chili-garlic sauce can be found in the Asian foods section.

Serves 4

Turkey, Stuffing, and Cranberry Sauce

Perfect for those holiday leftovers, but too tasty to neglect the rest of the year.

4 spinach tortillas
4 ounces (112 g) cream cheese
⅓ cup (90 g) cranberry sauce
1 cup (200 g) turkey stuffing
4 pieces turkey meat, white or dark
1 bunch arugula, washed and dried

- Heat the tortillas for a few seconds so they are pliable, then lay them out on a clean, dry work surface.

- With a spatula, spread cream cheese on each, then add cranberry sauce and stuffing. Top with a piece of turkey and a few leaves of the arugula. Roll up and serve.

Serves 4

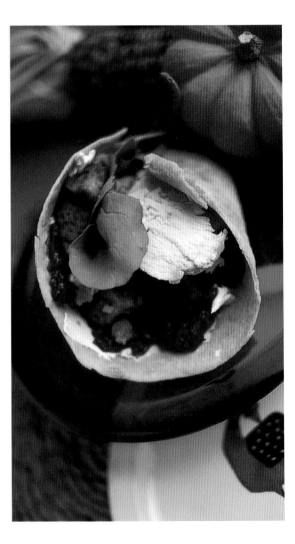

Chipotle, Sweet Potato, and Pork

You'll love the complementary flavors of this trio, but don't be afraid to substitute. May we suggest red potatoes with shredded leftover pot roast?

2 small sweet potatoes, boiled, peeled, and diced
2 teaspoons puréed chipotle pepper
2 cloves garlic, mashed
salt and freshly ground pepper
4 flour tortillas
½ pound (228 g) pork tenderloin, cooked and shredded
1 cup (4 ounces; 112 g) grated Monterey Jack cheese
1 bunch arugula, washed and dried

- Preheat the oven to 350°F (175°C).

- In a bowl or food processor, combine the sweet potatoes, chipotle, garlic, and salt and pepper to taste. Purée until smooth, adding a small amount of water if too thick.

- Heat the tortillas for a few seconds so they are pliable, then lay them out on a clean, dry work surface. Spread the sweet-potato mixture on each, then add the pork, cheese, and a few leaves of arugula.

- Roll up, put on a baking sheet, and place in the oven until the cheese melts.

Serves 4

Jambon and Cheese Crepes

A break from cereal on those days when a more leisurely breakfast can be enjoyed.

Crepes:
1 cup (112 g) flour
pinch of salt
1 egg
1 egg yolk
1¼ cup (300 ml) milk
1 tablespoon melted butter or oil
2–3 tablespoons oil

8 large slices (about 8 ounces; 228 g) ham
8 slices (about 7 ounces; 200 g) Gruyère cheese

- Preheat the oven to 350°F (175°C).

- *Make the crepes:* Sift the flour with a good pinch of salt into a mixing bowl. Make a well in the center. Whisk the egg, egg yolk, milk, and butter together. Slowly pour the egg mixture into the well of the flour while drawing in the sides with a fork. Stir until flour is just moistened; be careful not to overmix. Cover and set aside for 30 minutes.

- After resting, the batter should be the consistency of heavy cream. If it's too thick, gently stir in a teaspoon of water at a time until it reaches the desired consistency. Heat a 7-inch (18-cm) nonstick frying pan over medium-high heat, then add 1 tablespoon of oil. When the oil is hot, drop a few tablespoons of batter in the middle of the pan and swirl the pan around to make a solid crepe. Place the pan back on the heat until the underside of the crepe browns. Turn over and brown the other side. As you remove the crepes from the pan, place them on a wire rack on top of each other. Add more oil to the pan as necessary.

- Lay out 8 crepes and place a slice of ham and a slice of cheese on each one. Roll up and place in a baking dish. Heat in the oven until the cheese melts.

Serves 4

Scrambled Eggs and Black Beans with Red Pepper Sauce

A fun brunch dish that is colorful and delicious, these eggs are easy to prepare with ingredients you can keep on hand in your pantry and refrigerator.

Sauce:

1 sweet red pepper, broiled, peeled and seeded (see Note)

2 teaspoons herbes de Provence, or fines herbes (available in the spice section of the super-market)

salt and pepper

½ cup (120 ml) chicken stock (if required, to thin)

6 eggs

salt and pepper

1 tablespoon butter

four 8-inch (20-cm) tortillas (blue corn if available)

whole black beans, rinsed and drained (use a portion of a 15-ounce/425-g can)

½ cup (2 ounces; 55 g) grated pepper Jack cheese

- Preheat the oven to 300°F (150°C) and set a medium-size skillet on to heat.

- *Make the sauce:* Place the pepper in a blender with the herbs and salt and pepper to taste; purée until smooth. Heat in a small saucepan. If sauce is too thick, add chicken stock, a tablespoon at a time, until desired consistency is reached.

- Whisk the eggs to blend. Add salt and pepper to taste. Melt the butter in the skillet, then pour in the eggs. Using a wooden spoon, stir gently until eggs are just cooked.

- Divide the eggs evenly among the tortillas, then place 3 table-spoons of beans on each tortilla. (Reserve the leftover beans for another use.) Sprinkle with the cheese and roll up like a burrito. Place in a warm oven to melt the cheese. Remove from oven, spoon sauce over top, and serve.

Note: Broil the pepper(s), turning until black all over. Place in a bowl, cover with plastic wrap (cling film), and leave until cool. This will loosen the skin. Cut in half, peel, devein, and seed.

Serves 4

Egg, Prosciutto, and Asparagus

Here's another dish that is great for
a brunch and easy to prepare.

4 eggs
2 tablespoons grated Parmesan
  cheese
1 tablespoon chopped fresh
  oregano (3 tablespoons dried)
½ teaspoon salt
¼ teaspoon pepper
6–10 asparagus spears, trimmed
1 tablespoon plus ½ tablespoon
  butter
4 thin slices (about 2 ounces; 55 g)
  prosciutto

- In a bowl, whisk the eggs, Parmesan, oregano, salt, and pepper.

- Pour about 1 inch (2½ cm) water into a 9-inch (23-cm) nonstick pan and bring to a boil. Place the asparagus in the pan for 3–5 minutes or until just tender. Remove the asparagus and set aside.

- Throw out the water and place the pan back on the heat. Add the tablespoon of butter. When the butter has melted, pour in the egg mixture. Allow the eggs to cook about 2 minutes. Slide the "egg crepe" onto a cutting board.

- Place the asparagus and the prosciutto on the egg crepe and roll up. As you roll it up, spread the remaining ½ tablespoon of butter on the last edge of the crepe to seal. Cut in half and serve.

Serves 2

Pickled Garlic, Cheese, and Sun-dried Tomato

An attractive and easy hors d'oeuvre, but you'll want to plan well in advance.

½ cup (120 ml) plain yogurt
3 ounces (85 g) cream cheese
salt and pepper
three 8-inch (20-cm) whole-wheat
    tortillas
15 sun-dried tomatoes packed in
    oil, drained and sliced thin
¼ cup (15 g) fresh parsley, coarsely
    chopped
20 cloves pickled garlic, sliced in
    half

- Stir the yogurt, then place it in a fine-mesh strainer over a bowl. Place in the refrigerator and allow to drain for several hours, until all liquid is drained.

- Discard the liquid in the bowl. Take the contents of the strainer, "yogurt cheese," and mix together with the cream cheese until smooth. Salt and pepper to taste.

- Lay out the tortillas on a clean, dry work surface and spread them with the cheese mixture. Sprinkle on the tomatoes, parsley, and garlic. Roll up tight and refrigerate for several hours, overnight if desired.

- Slice the rolled tortillas into ½-inch (1-cm) slices, place on a platter, and serve.

Note: You can keep yogurt cheese on hand for many uses. Pickled garlic is available at the supermarket.

Makes 24 pieces

Asparagus, Cheese, and Prosciutto

Serve this when asparagus is in season. It's good for brunch, lunch, or as an hors d'oeuvre for a party.

1 pound (454 g) asparagus, trimmed
½ cup (2 ounces; 55 g) crumbled Gorgonzola cheese
2 tablespoons heavy cream
7 slices prosciutto (about ¼ pound; 112g), each cut into four pieces

- Place the asparagus in a sauté pan with enough water to cover and cook for approximately 1 minute (the asparagus should be bright green and still crisp). Remove the asparagus from the pan and plunge into cold water to stop cooking. Drain thoroughly.

- Stir the Gorgonzola and the cream together until smooth.

- On a clean, dry work surface lay out the quarter slices of prosciutto. With a small spatula or knife, spread the cheese mixture thinly over each piece. Place one asparagus at the end of each prosciutto piece and roll up.

- Place on a platter and serve.

Makes 28 pieces

Ravioli with Three Cheeses and Walnut Sauce

Rich, but oh so good!

Filling:
1 cup (4 ounces; 112 g) grated
    mozzarella cheese
1 cup (4 ounces; 112 g) Gorgonzola
    cheese
2 tablespoons freshly grated
    Parmesan cheese
1 egg, lightly beaten
1 tablespoon chopped chives or
    scallion

24 wonton wrappers

Sauce:
4 tablespoons unsalted butter
½ cup (60 g) coarsely chopped
    walnuts
½ cup (2 ounces; 55 g) freshly
    grated Parmesan cheese
salt and freshly grated pepper

- *Make the filling:* Mix the mozzarella, Gorgonzola, Parmesan, egg, and chives in a bowl and place in the refrigerator until ready to use.

- In a large pot, bring 4 quarts (4 l) of salted water to a rolling boil.

- On half of the wrappers, place 1 tablespoon of filling in the center of each. Lightly brush the edges of each square with cold water. Cover the filled halves with the remaining squares, pinching to seal the edges so they will not open while cooking.

- Carefully drop the "ravioli" into the pot, three at a time. As soon as the water returns to a boil, lower the heat to about medium and boil gently until tender, about 5 minutes.

- *Make the sauce:* Melt the butter in a large sauté pan, add the walnuts and sauté until the butter is lightly browned and the walnuts are golden.

- Drain the ravioli and add to the sauce, coating each piece well. Place in a serving dish, sprinkle with Parmesan, salt, and pepper, and serve.

Makes 24 pieces

Shrimp in Rice Paper

This might be one of the easiest and quickest hors d'oeuvres ever made. Also pretty and good to eat!

12 sheets rice paper *(bánh tráng)*
12 cilantro leaves plus extra stems for garnish
12 medium raw shrimp, washed, peeled, and deveined

- Trim each sheet of rice paper to a 4 × 5-inch (10 × 13-cm) rectangle. In a bowl of warm water, soak the sheets one at a time, until just pliable. Lay out on a clean towel.

- Place 1 cilantro leaf in the middle of each rectangle and cover with 1 shrimp. Fold the edges up around it to form a square.

- Place the squares in a lightly oiled dish that fits in your steamer basket. Place the steamer in a pan of boiling water, cover, and cook just until the shrimp have turned pink.

- Serve on a platter, garnished with stems of cilantro.

Makes 12 pieces

Shrimp and Pork Fried Wontons

These tasty morsels are a real treat. They can be prepared and frozen to be ready to fry for an almost instant hors d'oeuvre.

Filling:
¾ pound (340 g) small shrimp, rinsed, shelled, and deveined
¼ pound (112 g) ground pork
1 egg white, lightly beaten
1 teaspoon sugar
½ teaspoon salt
1 tablespoon grated fresh ginger
3 tablespoons dry sherry
1 tablespoon cornstarch
2 teaspoons sesame oil
4 tablespoons chopped scallions
freshly ground pepper

2 packages wonton wrappers
corn oil for frying

- Mix all the filling ingredients in a bowl and refrigerate, covered tightly with plastic wrap (cling film), for at least 30 minutes.

- Lay out the wonton wrappers on a clean, dry work surface with points toward you.

- Place 1 teaspoon of filling on the lower half of each wrapper. With a brush, moisten the edges with water. Fold the wrapper in half over the filling to form a triangle and thoroughly seal the edges. Fold the two side points over the filled middle, moisten them with water, and pinch to seal (see page 17).

- In a saucepan, heat approximately 3 inches (7.5 cm) of oil until the corner of a wonton sizzles when tested. Add a few at a time and fry until golden brown. Drain on a paper towel.

- Serve while still hot with your favorite dipping sauce.

Makes approximately 96 pieces

Vegetarian Spring Rolls

These egg rolls are not as quickly prepared as other dishes but are always appreciated by guests and family.

¼ cup (5 g) dried shitake mushrooms
2 teaspoons corn oil
½ pound (228 g) white ribs of bok choy, cut into ¼-inch (5-mm) cubes
1 scallion, trimmed
5 ounces (140 g) tofu, squeezed out thoroughly and crumbled
¼ cup (15 g) bean sprouts
1 carrot, peeled and grated
½ cup (55 g) water chestnuts, coarsely chopped
¼ cup (15 g) cilantro, coarsely chopped
2 cloves garlic, minced
2 teaspoons ginger juice (minced ginger squeezed through cheesecloth)
1½ tablespoons soy sauce
1 tablespoon cornstarch
1 package egg roll wrappers
egg wash (see Note)
oil for frying

- Soak mushrooms in 2 cups warm water for 30 minutes. Drain and chop coarsely.

- Heat the corn oil in a wok over medium heat. Add the bok choy and sauté until tender but still crisp. Set aside in a bowl.

- Thinly slice the scallion and add to the bok choy, along with the mushrooms, tofu, bean sprouts, carrot, water chestnuts, cilantro, garlic, ginger juice, and soy sauce.

- Mix the cornstarch with 1½ tablespoons of water and drizzle into the wok. Stir until mixture becomes glossy and holds together. Set aside to cool.

- On a clean, dry work surface, place 6 wrappers with the points facing you. Place ½ cup (55 g) of the vegetable mixture on the lower part of the wrapper and roll up, tucking in the sides as you go. Brush the end with egg wash to seal (see page 12).

- Put about 3 inches (7.5 cm) of oil in a wok and heat until the end of an egg roll sizzles when dipped briefly. Cook as many at a time as will comfortably fit in the wok. Fry until golden and drain on paper towels.

- Serve with your favorite dipping sauce.

Note: To make an egg wash, whisk 1 egg with 1 tablespoon of water.

Makes 6 egg rolls

Smoked Salmon Roulade

This simple roulade serves many guests with a minimum of preparation.

3 ounces (85 g) cream cheese
2 tablespoons mayonnaise
2 tablespoons fresh lemon juice
2 teaspoons minced red onion
1 teaspoon dill
1 tablespoon capers, drained and
  chopped
8 ounces (228 g) smoked salmon,
  nova style
3 teaspoons chopped parsley
1 package Carr's Table Water
  Crackers

- Mix the cream cheese with the mayonnaise, lemon juice, onion, dill, and capers.

- Lay out a piece of plastic wrap (cling film) and place the slices of salmon on it in overlapping rows, creating a rectangle with the long side facing you. Sprinkle with the chopped parsley and spread with the cheese mixture.

- Roll up, beginning from the long side. Use the plastic wrap to keep the layers together. When rolled, seal tightly in the wrap and place in the refrigerator overnight or until completely chilled.

- Remove from the refrigerator and slice about $3/8$ inch (1 cm) thick. Place each slice on a cracker and serve immediately.

Makes approximately 24 pieces

Goat Cheese and Spicy Meat Empanadas

An excellent hors d'oeuvre to pass around at your next party.

1 pound (454 g) ground beef
1 tablespoon chopped garlic
½ bunch parsley, chopped
1½ tablespoons chili-garlic sauce
    (see Note)
salt and pepper
8 sheets puff pastry, rolled out to
    ¼-inch (6-mm) thickness
4 ounces (112 g) goat cheese
egg wash (see Note, page 38)

- Preheat the oven to 400°F (200°C).

- Sauté the ground beef in a skillet until brown. Add the garlic and continue cooking for 2 minutes. Drain off and discard any fat.

- Place in a bowl and mix in the parsley, chili-garlic sauce, and salt and pepper to taste.

- Lay out the pastry on a lightly floured board and cut into 4-inch (10 cm) rounds using an upside-down glass or cookie cutter.

- Place a small amount of the meat mixture on one side of each round and top with a bit of cheese. Brush egg wash around the outer edge of each pastry. Fold each round in half, press the edges together, and crimp with a fork.

- Bake for 25 minutes or until brown and puffy.

Note: Chili-garlic sauce can be found in the Asian foods section of the supermarket.

Makes approximately 48 pieces

Ground Beef in Phyllo

This relatively simple recipe can be easily doubled to feed more guests.

Filling:
1 tablespoon butter
½ cup (85 g) finely chopped onion
½ pound (228 g) ground round
   steak
2 tablespoons dry white wine
6 tablespoons tomato paste
salt and freshly ground pepper
1 tablespoon grated Parmesan
   cheese
1 egg, beaten

6 sheets phyllo pastry
¼ cup (60 ml) butter, melted

- *Make the filling:* In a small sauté pan, melt the butter, then add the onion and 1 tablespoon of water. Cook, stirring, until the liquid evaporates. Add the steak and cook, breaking up the lumps with a fork, until the meat just loses its red color.

- Add the wine and cook until it comes to a boil. Add the tomato paste and salt and pepper to taste. Cover and cook over low heat for about 15 minutes. Remove from heat, uncover, and let cool slightly. Stir in cheese and egg and set aside to cool.

- Preheat the oven to 350°F (175°C).

- Working with one sheet at a time, lay out the phyllo on a clean, dry work surface. Brush with butter, then cut vertically into four equal strips.

- Place 2 teaspoons of the filling on the end nearest you and roll up, turning in the ends as you go. Place the roll on a baking sheet and continue with the rest of the strips until the filling and pastry are used up. Butter the top of each roll and place in the oven. Bake 15 to 20 minutes or until golden.

Makes 24 pieces

Spinach-Almond Empanadas

These pastries have a delicious filling and are excellent warm or at room temperature.

Béchamel sauce:
1 tablespoon butter
1 tablespoon flour
½ cup (120 ml) milk

Filling:
one-half 10-ounce (285-g) package
    frozen chopped spinach, thawed
1 tablespoon butter
½ onion, finely diced
1¼ cups (5 ounces; 140 g) grated
    Monterey Jack cheese
salt and freshly ground pepper
¼ teaspoon nutmeg
½ cup (80 g) whole almonds,
    toasted and coarsely chopped
¼ cup (25 g) currants
1 sheet puff pastry
egg wash (see Note, page 38)

- *Make the béchamel sauce:* Melt the butter in a small saucepan but do not brown. Add the flour and stir until smooth. Add the milk all at once and stir until thickened.

- By the handful or using a cheesecloth, squeeze the moisture from the spinach.

- Melt the butter in a small sauté pan and add the onion. Sauté on low heat until translucent. Add the spinach to the pan and mix thoroughly.

- In a large bowl, combine the béchamel sauce, spinach mixture, cheese, salt and pepper to taste, nutmeg, almonds, and currants.

- Preheat the oven to 350°F (175°C).

- Lay out the sheet of puff pastry on a lightly floured board. Cut pastry into 3½-inch (9-cm) rounds using an upside-down glass or cookie cutter. Place a rounded teaspoon of filling on one side of each round. Brush egg wash around the outer edge of each pastry. Fold each round in half, press the edges together, and crimp with a fork.

- Place the filled pastries on a sheet pan lined with parchment paper. Brush the tops with the remaining egg wash and place in the oven. Bake until golden brown (about 15 minutes). Serve hot or at room temperature.

Serves 4

Sweet Peppers and Black Beans with Arugula, Mango, and Avocado Salad

Colorful peppers, black beans, avocados, and sweet mangoes— an irresistible combination!

1 sweet red pepper, seeded
1 sweet yellow pepper, seeded
1 small red onion
¼ cup (60 ml) plus 2 tablespoons lemon juice
¼ teaspoon plus ¼ teaspoon red pepper flakes
salt and freshly ground pepper
one 15-ounce (425 g) can black beans, rinsed and drained
¼ teaspoon cumin
¼ teaspoon coriander
¼ cup (60 ml) plus 2 tablespoons olive oil
1 bunch arugula, washed and dried
1 mango, peeled and sliced
1 avocado, peeled and sliced
two 9-inch (23-cm) whole-wheat tortillas

- Using a fine grater or food processor, shave the red and yellow peppers and the onion.

- Combine the peppers, onion, the ¼ cup (60 ml) of lemon juice, the ¼ teaspoon red pepper flakes, and salt and pepper to taste in a bowl, and refrigerate for 2 hours. Drain before using.

- In a food processor, purée the black beans, cumin, coriander, the remaining ¼ teaspoon red pepper flakes, the ¼ cup olive oil, and salt to taste, until smooth. Set aside.

- In a bowl, toss the arugula, mango, and avocado with the remaining 2 tablespoons lemon juice, 2 tablespoons oil, and salt and pepper to taste.

- Spread a layer of bean purée on each tortilla, cover with a thin layer of the pepper-onion mixture, and then add some of the arugula salad. Roll up each tortilla, trim the ends, cut in half, and serve.

Serves 2

Greek Salad with Hummus

This pita wrap combines favorite flavors from Greece and is fresh, crunchy, and tasty.

Salad (see Note):
2 roma tomatoes, cut into 8 pieces
    each
¼ cucumber, peeled, halved,
    seeded, and sliced into ¼-inch
    (5-mm) slices
¼ red onion, sliced thin
10 Mediterranean-style olives, such
    as kalamata, pitted and cut in
    half
¼ cup (1 ounce; 28 g) crumbled
    feta cheese
4 leaves iceberg lettuce

Dressing:
1 tablespoon lemon juice
½ teaspoon dry oregano
salt and freshly ground pepper
2 tablespoons extra-virgin olive oil

Hummus (see Note):
one 15-ounce (439-g) can garbanzo
    beans, drained
3 tablespoons tahini (a sesame seed
    paste available in most super-
    markets)

2 tablespoons olive oil
juice of 1 lemon
1 clove garlic
1 teaspoon cumin
salt and pepper

4 pita pockets

- *Make the salad:* Place all the salad ingredients in a bowl and set aside.

- *Make the dressing:* In a small bowl, place the lemon juice, oregano, and salt and pepper to taste. Whisk together, then slowly whisk in the oil. Toss with the salad.

- *Make the hummus:* Place all the hummus ingredients in a food processor and blend until smooth. If the mixture is too thick, add more oil or warm water.

- Warm the pita pockets in the oven for a few minutes. Cut the pita in half and spread several tablespoons of the hummus inside. Divide the salad into 8 portions and spoon inside the pita.

Note: For greater ease of preparation, purchase premade Greek salad, available at many supermarket deli counters. Hummus can also be bought ready-made.

Serves 4

Lentil and Sultana Salad

This is a simple, nutritious salad. It is best made ahead of time so that the diverse flavors blend together.

1 cup (200 g) brown lentils, washed and picked through
1½ tablespoons fresh lemon juice
1½ tablespoons olive oil
¾ cup (155 g) rice, cooked according to package instructions
1 medium red onion, finely chopped
½ cup (60 g) sultanas (golden raisins)
4 tablespoons Italian parsley, finely chopped
½ teaspoon salt
¼ teaspoon freshly ground pepper
4 naan bread

- Bring 2 cups (460 ml) of water to a boil and pour over the lentils in a large bowl. Let soak 1 hour, then drain. Transfer the lentils to a large saucepan, add 2 cups of water, and bring to a boil. Lower the heat and simmer, covered, until just tender, about 35 minutes. Drain and set aside.

- Whisk together the lemon juice and the oil. In a large bowl, combine the lentils, rice, onion, and sultanas, and mix thoroughly. Pour the lemon juice and oil over and mix well. Let stand, covered, in the refrigerator for at least 1 hour. Just before serving, add the parsley, salt, and pepper, and mix well.

- Warm the naan breads in the oven for a few minutes so they are pliable but not crisp. Place about 1 cup of the salad on each of the breads and roll up.

Serves 4

vegetarian

Roasted Vegetables

A delicious and nutritious lunch or light supper. Any vegetable can be substituted or added, like squash, mushrooms or potatoes. Your choice!

½ sweet red pepper, thinly sliced
½ red onion, thinly sliced
1 zucchini, thinly sliced
½ eggplant, sliced
3 tablespoons olive oil
1 tablespoon chopped garlic
salt and freshly ground pepper
1 pound (454 g) frozen pizza
    dough, thawed
¼ cup (65 g) pesto
½ cup (2 ounces; 55 g) shredded
    Parmesan cheese
½ cup shredded mozzarella cheese
egg wash (see Note, page 38)

- Preheat oven to 400°F (200°C).

- Toss the red pepper, onion, zucchini, and eggplant with the oil and garlic and place on a baking sheet. Sprinkle all over with salt and pepper and roast in the oven for 30 minutes or until the vegetables are cooked.

- Roll out the dough into 4 rounds, 8 inches (20 cm) in diameter and ⅛ inch (3 mm) thick.

- With a spatula, spread one tablespoon of pesto on each round. Divide the vegetables into 4 portions and place on the rounds. Sprinkle each round with Parmesan and mozzarella.

- Brush the edge of each round with egg wash. Fold the round in half over the vegetables and carefully seal the dough with your fingers. Place in the oven and cook until the dough is golden brown.

Serves 4

Brown Rice, Tofu, and Vegetables

A very healthy filling for pita bread. You can make a big batch to keep on hand for a quick lunch. Kids love it!

4 ounces (112 g) tofu
½ small onion
1 small carrot
1 stalk celery
1 small zucchini and/or other
    summer squash
3 ounces (82 g) mushrooms
2 stalks broccoli flowerettes
1 tablespoon olive oil
1 tablespoon butter
2 cloves garlic, finely chopped
½ teaspoon cumin
salt
¼ cup (60 ml) vegetable stock,
    mushroom broth, or water
⅓ cup (65 g) brown rice, cooked
    according to package instruc-
    tions
¾ cup (3 ounces; 82 g) grated
    Monterey Jack cheese
pepper
4 pita pockets
8 leaves red leaf lettuce
fresh herbs for garnish

- Drain the tofu while you prepare the vegetables.

- Dice the onion, carrot, celery, and zucchini into ½-inch (1-cm) cubes. Quarter the mushrooms if small, or cut them into sixths or eighths if large. Cut the broccoli into small pieces. Dice the tofu into ½-inch (1-cm) cubes.

- Preheat the oven to 350°F (175°C).

- In a large sauté pan, heat the olive oil and butter. Sauté the onions until they are lightly browned. Add the garlic, cumin, and a large pinch of salt, and cook for 1 minute. Add the carrots and celery. Add 2 tablespoons of the vegetable stock, cover the pan, and braise the vegetables for about 5 minutes or until they begin to soften. Add the zucchini, mushrooms, and broccoli and cook another 7–10 minutes. The vegetables should not be completely cooked. Add more stock if the vegetables get too dry.

- Combine the vegetables with the rice and cheese and season liberally with salt and pepper. Fold in the tofu and place in a lightly oiled or buttered baking dish. Moisten with a little more liquid if necessary. Cover the pan with foil and bake for 30 minutes. Remove from the oven.

- Cut the pita pockets in half and fill each with rice mixture. Line each plate with 2 lettuce leaves and place 2 pita halves on each plate. Garnish with fresh herbs and serve.

Serves 4

Lobster Salad

This combination of fresh fruits and seafood can't be beat. You can substitute other seafood if lobster is out of your reach.

Salad:
cooked meat of 1 lobster (see
    Note), cut into 1-inch (2.5-cm)
    cubes, or ½ pound (228 g) other
    seafood
1 small papaya, cubed
3 roma tomatoes, diced
1 orange, peeled and sectioned
4 scallions, thinly sliced

Dressing:
2 tablespoons fresh orange juice
2 teaspoons red wine vinegar
1 teaspoon grated fresh ginger
2 teaspoons Dijon mustard
½ tablespoon honey
salt and freshly ground pepper
⅓ cup (80 ml) olive oil

2 large heads radicchio

- *Make the salad:* Place all the salad ingredients in a bowl and set aside.

- *Make the dressing:* In a small bowl, place the orange juice, vinegar, ginger, mustard, and honey and salt and pepper to taste. Whisk together, then slowly whisk in the oil. Toss with the salad.

- Peel off several radicchio leaves. Using the 8 largest leaves, place approximately ⅓ cup of salad on each. Fold up the bottom of the leaf and then fold over the sides and roll up.

Note: Check with your local seafood store; lobster meat is often available fresh, or you can use frozen.

Serves 2

Caesar Salad with Crab

A mouth-watering lunch for any occasion!

6 tablespoons mayonnaise
1 small garlic clove, finely chopped
2 anchovy fillets, finely chopped
pinch paprika
1½ tablespoons grated Parmesan cheese
salt and freshly grated pepper
one lavash, or "soft cracker bread"
6 leaves romaine lettuce
¾ pound (340 g) cooked crab meat
1 scallion, thinly sliced
¼ cup (35 g) celery, finely chopped
2 thin slices red onion
¼ lemon

- Preheat the oven to 300°F (150°C).

- In a small bowl, mix together the mayonnaise, garlic, anchovies, paprika, and Parmesan. Add salt and pepper to taste.

- Spread the mayonnaise mixture on the lavash, then place the lettuce leaves on the bread and cover with the crab meat. Sprinkle with the scallion, celery, and red onion. Squeeze lemon juice over the crab and roll up. Cut into 2-inch (5-cm) slices and serve.

Serves 2

Fresh Tuna with Jicama and Carrot Salad

This sophisticated burrito is healthy, delicious, and colorful.

1 pound (454 g) fresh sushi-quality
tuna steak
1 teaspoon salt
1 teaspoon coarsely ground pepper
6 tablespoons corn oil
6 jalapeño peppers, finely chopped
¾ cup (200 g) mayonnaise
¼ cup (60 ml) plus 2 tablespoons
lime juice
1 medium carrot, peeled and
julienned
1 small jicama, peeled and
julienned
¼ cup (60 ml) extra-virgin olive oil
1 tablespoon finely chopped
cilantro
1 tablespoon finely chopped fresh
thyme
four 9-inch (23-cm) whole-wheat
tortillas
½ cup (25 g) arugula leaves

- Slice the tuna into ½-inch (1 cm) strips and marinate in a bowl with the salt, pepper, and corn oil for five minutes.

- Mix the jalapeños with the mayonnaise and the ¼ cup (60 ml) lime juice and season with salt and pepper to taste.

- Dress the carrot and jicama with the olive oil, the 2 tablespoons lime juice, the cilantro, and the thyme and set aside in the refrigerator while you cook the tuna.

- Sear the marinated tuna strips on the grill or in a frying pan over high heat for 5 seconds on each side.

- Heat the tortillas in a warm oven just until soft but not crisp. Place the tortillas on a clean, dry work surface and spread mayonnaise mixture on each one. Drain the carrots and jicama, divide into four portions, and place on each tortilla, a little below center. Add two pieces of tuna and some arugula and roll up tightly. Cut each tortilla in half and serve.

Serves 4

Tomato Tortillas with Black Beans, Guacamole, and Trout

Smoked trout added to this South of the Border treat makes it a true fusion delight.

2 cups (350 g) cooked black beans
    or 1½ cans (15-ounce; 425 g)
    black beans, rinsed and drained
¼ teaspoon cumin
¼ teaspoon coriander
2 ripe avocados
2 serrano chilies, finely chopped
½ red onion, finely chopped
2 tablespoons fresh lime juice
1 smoked trout fillet, about 5
    ounces (140 g)
one 14-inch (35.5-cm) tomato
    tortilla

- Purée half the beans in a food processor with the cumin and coriander. Place the puréed beans in a bowl and fold in the remaining, whole, beans. Set aside.

- Peel and pit the avocados and mash them with the back of a fork until they are almost smooth but still have some texture. Add the serranos, red onion, and lime juice.

- Place the tortilla on a clean, dry work surface and, with a spatula, spread a generous amount of the bean mixture over the entire tortilla. Spread the guacamole mixture over the beans. Lay finger-sized pieces of trout in a single row on the lower half of the tortilla. Roll up and cut into ¾-inch (2-cm) slices.

Serves 4

Spicy Shrimp

This dish incorporates the flavors of India. Curry leaves can be found at Indian or Asian markets. Uncooked shrimp can be purchased shelled and deveined with the tails on in the freezer section of your supermarket.

¼ cup (60 ml) canola oil
1 teaspoon mustard seeds
20 curry leaves
1 teaspoon grated fresh ginger
3 small garlic cloves, mashed
2 cups (360 g) chopped onions
½ teaspoon turmeric
pinch cayenne
½ cup (115 g) peeled, seeded, and
    chopped tomatoes (see Note)
salt and freshly ground black
    pepper
20 medium shrimp (about
    ¾ pound; 340 g), peeled
    and deveined
4 pieces naan bread
chopped cilantro for garnish

- In a large sauté pan, heat the oil and add the mustard seeds and curry leaves, cooking until brown. Add the ginger and garlic paste and cook until golden. Add the onions and cook and stir for 5 minutes. Stir in the turmeric, cayenne, tomatoes, and salt and black pepper to taste and cook for another 2 minutes. Add the shrimp and cook, stirring, until they are opaque, about 3 minutes more.

- Divide the shrimp mixture into 4 portions, place one portion on the end of each naan bread, and roll. Garnish with the cilantro.

Note: To peel the tomatoes, bring 1 quart of water to boil in a saucepan. Drop in the tomatoes and leave 30 seconds. Remove with a slotted spoon.

Serves 4

Fresh Tuna Ravioli

This is a great dish for a starter or an entrée.

Filling:
½ pound (228 g) fresh tuna, finely
    ground
1 egg yolk
8 leaves fresh tarragon, chopped
½ teaspoon grated fresh ginger
4 ounces (112 g) ricotta
salt and pepper

1 package wonton wrappers
egg wash (see Note, page 38)
1 cup finely julienned fresh ginger
1 cup (230 ml) vegetable oil

Sauce:
2 tablespoons olive oil
2 cups peeled, seeded, and chopped
    tomatoes (see Note, page 61)
8 leaves fresh tarragon
2 cloves garlic, minced
salt and pepper

2 tablespoons butter

- *Make the filling:* In a bowl, combine the tuna, egg yolk, tarragon, ginger, and ricotta. Add salt and pepper to taste.

- On a clean, dry work surface, lay out 32 wonton wrappers. Place 1 tablespoon of filling on each wrapper. Brush egg wash around the edges. Cover each square with a fresh wrapper, pressing around the mound to seal completely.

- Fry the julienned ginger in the vegetable oil until golden and crispy, about 1 minute. Drain on paper towels and set aside.

- *Make the sauce:* In a frying pan, heat the olive oil and add the tomatoes and tarragon. Add the garlic and salt and pepper to taste and simmer slowly for about 5 minutes.

- Bring a large pot of salted water to boil. Carefully drop in the ravioli and cook for about 3 minutes. With a slotted spoon, remove the ravioli from the water and add to the sauce. Fold in the butter and cook for another minute or two. Garnish with the fried ginger threads and serve.

Serves 8

Smoked Chicken and Gouda with Barbecue Sauce and Cilantro

An uncomplicated treat for impromptu visits.

1 pound (454 g) frozen pizza
    dough, thawed
1 cup (230 ml) barbecue sauce
2 smoked chicken breasts, cubed
4 slices (about 8 ounces; 228 g)
    smoked gouda
1 red onion, thinly sliced
1 bunch cilantro, coarsely chopped
1 tablespoon coarse cornmeal

- Preheat the oven to 450°F (230°C).

- Divide the dough into quarters and roll each quarter into a round, 8 inches (20 cm) in diameter and ⅛ inch (3 mm) thick.

- Cover each round evenly with barbecue sauce, leaving at least 1 inch (2.5 cm) on each side. Sprinkle the chicken over the sauce. Top with cheese, onion, and cilantro.

- Place pizzas on a cookie sheet sprinkled lightly with cornmeal. Bake for 15 minutes or until browned on the bottom.

- Remove from the oven and allow to cool slightly. Roll up and serve.

Serves 4

Curried Duck with Rice and Parsley-Mint Sauce

Duck gives this dish its distinctive flavor.

Sauce:
½ cup (120 ml) extra-virgin olive oil
¼ cup (60 ml) fresh lemon juice
2 teaspoons minced garlic
½ cup (30 g) chopped Italian parsley
½ cup (55 g) minced shallots
¼ cup (15 g) slivered mint leaves
salt and cayenne pepper

Curried duck:
2 tablespoons olive oil
¾ cup (80 g) chopped onions
4 large cloves garlic, minced
2 teaspoons minced fresh ginger
1 whole duck breast poached, cooled, and shredded
2 tablespoons curry powder
2 teaspoons cumin
1 teaspoon coriander
⅓ cup (180 ml) chicken broth
salt and freshly ground black pepper
2 tablespoons chopped cilantro

⅓ cup (65 g) rice, cooked according to package instructions

¼ cup (30 g) scallions, thinly sliced
¼ cup (30 g) raisins, plumped in warm water and drained
¼ cup (40 g) slivered almonds, toasted
four 8-inch (20-cm) whole-wheat tortillas
1 bunch arugula, washed and dried

- *Make the sauce:* In a medium bowl combine the olive oil, lemon juice, garlic, parsley, shallots, and mint. Season with salt and cayenne to taste and set aside for about an hour to let the flavors develop.

- *Make the curried duck:* In a large sauté pan, heat the olive oil, then add the onions, garlic, and ginger, stirring until the onions are soft and light brown. Stir in the duck meat, curry powder, cumin, and coriander and cook, stirring, for about 5 minutes, until the meat is lightly browned. Add the chicken broth and cook, stirring occasionally, until the liquid has evaporated. Season with salt and black pepper to taste and set aside to cool. When cooled, stir in the cilantro.

- Combine the rice with the scallions, raisins, and almonds.

- Preheat the oven to 350ºF (175ºC).

- Place one-fourth of the rice mixture on each of the tortillas. Top with one-fourth of the curried duck. Add several leaves of arugula to each, and roll. Place on a baking sheet and warm in the oven for about 5 minutes. Remove from the oven and serve with the sauce on the side.

Serves 4

Chicken Salad with Curry Lime Mayo, Cashews, and Mango

An exotic twist to traditional chicken salad.

2 tablespoons olive oil
2½ teaspoons curry powder
2 tablespoons fresh lime juice
2 tablespoons mango chutney, roughly chopped
1 cup (250 g) mayonnaise
¼ cup (15 g) shredded unsweetened coconut
1 whole chicken breast, poached, cooled, and shredded
½ cup (70 g) cashews, coarsely chopped
2 tablespoons currants
1 mango, peeled and cut into cubes
four 8-inch (20-cm) whole-wheat tortillas

- In a small frying pan, heat the oil. Add the curry powder and stir until it begins to foam and become fragrant. Set aside to cool.

- In a bowl, mix the lime juice, chutney, mayonnaise, and cooled curry paste.

- Toast the coconut in an ungreased frying pan or in the oven until golden, and allow to cool.

- Combine the mayonnaise mixture with the chicken, coconut, cashews, currants, and mango and stir to distribute the dressing evenly.

- Lay out the tortillas on a clean, dry work surface and place one-fourth of the filling on each tortilla. Roll up and serve.

Serves 4

Chicken Tikka

Plan ahead to serve this simple, delicious, and colorful chicken, with a healthy low-fat cooling sauce.

Marinade:
juice of ½ lemon
½ tablespoon turmeric
1 tablespoon chopped fresh ginger
2 large cloves garlic
1 teaspoon paprika
1 teaspoon coriander
1 teaspoon cumin
salt and freshly ground pepper
⅓ cup (80 ml) plain low-fat yogurt

1 whole boneless, skinless chicken
    breast, split

Raita:
½ cup (115 g) peeled, seeded, and
    finely diced cucumber
½ cup (115 g) peeled, seeded,
    and diced tomato (see Note,
    page 61)
1 cup (230 ml) plain low-fat yogurt
salt and freshly ground pepper

4 whole-wheat pita pockets

- *Make the marinade:* Blend the lemon juice, turmeric, ginger, garlic, paprika, coriander, cumin, and salt and pepper to taste in a blender or food processor. Add the yogurt and mix thoroughly with a fork.

- Marinate the chicken in the mixture for approximately 12 hours.

- *Make the raita:* Combine the cucumber, tomato, and yogurt and salt and pepper to taste.

- Grill the marinated chicken under the broiler for 4 minutes on each side until opaque. Slice thinly, lengthwise.

- Cut the tops off the pita pockets. Fill with chicken and raita and serve.

Serves 4

B'steeya

This combination of chicken, cinnamon, orange, and ginger is oh, so good!

2 onions, finely chopped
1 tablespoon butter
1 teaspoon grated fresh ginger
1 teaspoon cinnamon
1 whole boneless chicken breast,
    poached, cooled, and shredded
3 tablespoons chopped parsley
2 tablespoons chopped cilantro
2 tablespoons currants
grated rind of 1 orange
1 egg
salt and freshly ground pepper
1 package phyllo pastry
½ cup (112 g) butter, melted

- Preheat the oven to 350°F (175°C).

- Sauté the onion in the butter until translucent. Add the ginger and cinnamon, and cook a minute or so longer. Turn out into a bowl.

- Add the chicken to the onions along with the parsley, cilantro, currants, and orange rind. Whisk the egg and stir it through. Season with salt and pepper to taste.

- Lay out a sheet of phyllo and brush it with butter. Top with another sheet, butter, and continue in the same manner until you have layered three sheets of pastry. Cut vertically into four pieces. Place one-fourth of the filling on one end of the pastry and fold it like a flag (see directions for flag fold, page 14). Repeat for the remaining pieces. Brush each piece with butter. Place on an ungreased baking sheet and bake for about 30 minutes or until slightly puffed and light brown.

Serves 4

Cold Roast Lamb and Tapenade

Here's a taste of Greece—with lamb and olives added to a fresh crunchy salad.

Tapenade:
½ cup (60 g) Mediterranean-style olives, such as kalamata, pitted and cut in half
2 anchovy fillets
1 tablespoon capers, drained
1 clove garlic
¼ cup (15 g) chopped Italian parsley
1 teaspoon pepper
3 tablespoons olive oil

½ pound (228 g) leg of lamb, rubbed with garlic and oil, roasted, and refrigerated overnight or until cold
4 whole-wheat pita pockets
4 leaves romaine lettuce
8 slices beefsteak tomato
4 slices red onion

- *Make the tapenade:* Place the olives, anchovies, capers, garlic, parsley, and pepper in a food processor fitted with a steel blade. Turn on the machine, pour in the oil, and process until the ingredients form a smooth paste.

- Cut the lamb into thin slices.

- Warm the pita pockets in the oven for a few minutes, then remove and cut ½ inch (1.2 cm) off the top of each. Spread the inside liberally with the tapenade and stuff with lettuce, tomato, onion, and several slices of lamb.

Note: For a shortcut, purchase tapenade at the supermarket deli counter.

Serves 4

Lavash with Ham and Pesto Mayonnaise

A lunch to pack for work, serve at the table, send off to school with the kids, or take on a picnic!

1 cup (250 g) mayonnaise
2 tablespoons pesto
2 lavash, or "soft cracker bread"
1 bunch red leaf lettuce, washed and dried
1 red onion, thinly sliced
5 tomatoes, sliced
1 pound (454 g) smoked ham, thinly sliced

- Mix the mayonnaise and pesto together. Spread evenly over each lavash. Cover each of the breads with lettuce and slices of onion, tomato, and ham. Roll up and slice into 2-inch (5-cm) sandwiches.

Serves 4

Stuffed Flank Steak

This dish makes a hearty meal or a very colorful presentation for your hors d'oeuvre table.

8 cups (230 g) fresh spinach, washed and trimmed
½ cup (65 g) dried bread crumbs
½ cup (2 ounces; 55 g) freshly grated Parmesan cheese
¼ cup (60 ml) olive oil
2 cloves garlic
1½ pounds (682 g) flank steak, butterflied
salt and freshly ground pepper
¼ pound (112 g) coppacola (a type of Italian ham), thinly sliced
3 sweet red peppers, broiled, peeled and seeded (see Note, page 26)

- Preheat the oven to 350°F (175°C).

- Place the spinach in a saucepan with just the water that clings to the leaves. Cover and cook over medium heat until just wilted, about five minutes. Drain in a colander, rinse with cold water to cool. By the handful or using a cheesecloth, squeeze out the moisture.

- In a food processor, combine the spinach, bread crumbs, Parmesan, olive oil, and garlic and purée until thick and smooth. Transfer to a bowl.

- Place the butterflied steak on a clean, dry work surface and season with salt and pepper to taste. Place the coppacola on the steak in a single layer, then add the peppers, outside surface down. Top with the spinach mixture, spreading it over the peppers.

- Starting with the long side, roll the steak up tightly. Tie with string at 2-inch (5-cm) intervals. Brush with olive oil, and season with salt and pepper. Place the steak in a roasting pan and cook for 40 minutes; the steak should be medium rare. If using as an entrée, let cool slightly, slice, and serve. If using as an hors d'oeuvre, cover and put in the refrigerator to chill thoroughly before slicing.

Serves 4

Pear, Ginger, and Currant Turnovers in Rice Paper

Any combination of fruit can be used here. I use pears with ginger and currants and a few almonds to give the turnovers some crunch.

Filling:
2 fresh pears, peeled, cored, and
    coarsely chopped
¼ cup (25 g) currants, plumped in
    warm water and drained
1 tablespoon grated fresh ginger
2 tablespoons slivered almonds
1 tablespoon granulated sugar
1 tablespoon unsalted butter,
    melted
2 tablespoons crème fraîche

¼ cup (50 g) granulated sugar
twelve 8-inch (20-cm) rounds rice
    paper *(bánh tráng)*
4 tablespoons unsalted butter

1 cup (240 ml) crème fraîche
1 tablespoon brown sugar

- Preheat the oven to 400°F (200°C).

- *Make the filling:* In a small bowl, mix the pears, currants, ginger, and almonds. Let stand for about 30 minutes. Stir in the 1 tablespoon granulated sugar, the 1 tablespoon melted butter, and the 2 tablespoons crème fraîche.

- Fill a large bowl with hot water. Add the ¼ cup (50 g) granulated sugar and stir to dissolve. Working with one round of rice paper at a time, immerse the paper in the water for about 2 seconds or until just pliable. Remove to a dry towel. Brush each paper with the melted butter. Place one-fourth of the filling on the lower half of each round and roll up, folding in the sides over the filling to form a square. Brush all over with melted butter. Place seam side down on a nonstick baking sheet.

- Bake for approximately 20 minutes or until crisp and golden. Mix the 1 cup crème fraîche and the brown sugar in a small bowl and serve on the side.

Serves 4

Chocolate Ravioli with Caramel Sauce

Here's a treat for chocoholics and just plain dessert lovers.

Pasta:
2 cups (224 g) flour
1 tablespoon confectioners' sugar
2 tablespoons cocoa
3 eggs
1 teaspoon oil

Filling:
8 ounces (228 g) mascarpone
1 teaspoon vanilla
¼ cup (55 g) chopped pistachios

Sauce:
1 cup (220 g) brown sugar
6 tablespoons butter
¼ cup (60 ml) heavy cream

egg wash (see Note, page 38)
¼ cup (55 g) chopped pistachios

- *Make the pasta:* Sift the flour, sugar, and cocoa onto a board. In a bowl, whisk the eggs and oil together. Make a well in the center of the flour and slowly pour in the eggs while drawing in the flour with a fork to make a dough. Knead well. Cover and allow to rest for 15 minutes.

- *Make the filling:* Mix the mascarpone with the vanilla and the ¼ cup (55 g) pistachios. Set aside.

- *Make the sauce:* Heat the brown sugar, butter, and cream over low heat. Stir constantly until the sugar melts, about 5–7 minutes. Allow to come to a boil. Stir.

- Roll out the pasta as thin as possible (preferably in a pasta machine). Lay strips over a drying rack or the back of a chair to dry, about 30 minutes. Using a 3½-inch (9-cm) cookie cutter, cut out 24 rounds.

- Lay out pasta rounds on a clean, dry work surface. Place about 1 tablespoon of filling on 12 of the rounds. Brush the egg wash completely around each mound of filling. Cover with the other 12 rounds and press the edges to seal.

- Bring 4 quarts (4 l) of water to a boil. Carefully drop half the ravioli in the water and reduce the heat. Allow to simmer for about 3 minutes, then lift out with a slotted spoon. Repeat with the remaining 6 pieces.

- Place a few ravioli on each plate. Spoon some of the caramel sauce over and sprinkle with the remaining ¼ cup (55 g) nuts. Serve hot.

Serves 4

Sautéed Apple and Cheddar Cheese Wrap

A simple, homey dessert wrap that's simple to prepare.

Crepes:
1 cup (112 g) flour
pinch of salt
1 egg
1 egg yolk
1¼ cups (300 ml) milk
1 tablespoon melted butter or oil
2–3 tablespoons oil

Filling:
4 tablespoons butter
2 apples, peeled, cored, and sliced
1 tablespoon sugar
1½ teaspoons cinnamon

1 cup (4 ounces; 112 g) grated
    cheddar cheese

- *Make the crepes:* Sift the flour with a good pinch of salt into a mixing bowl. Make a well in the center. Whisk the egg, egg yolk, milk, and butter together. Slowly pour the egg mixture into the well of the flour while drawing in the sides with a fork. Stir until flour is just moistened; be careful not to overmix. Cover and set aside for 30 minutes.

- After resting, the batter should be the consistency of heavy cream. If it's too thick, gently stir in a teaspoon of water at a time until it reaches the desired consistency. Heat a 7-inch (18-cm) nonstick frying pan over medium-high heat, then add 1 tablespoon of oil. When the oil is hot, drop a few tablespoons of batter in the middle of the pan and swirl the pan around to make a solid crepe. Place the pan back on the heat until the underside of the crepe browns. Turn over and brown the other side. As you remove the crepes from the pan, place them on a wire rack on top of each other. Add more oil to the pan as necessary.

- Preheat the oven to 350°F (175°C).

- *Make the filling:* Heat the butter in a sauté pan and add the apple slices. Cook over medium heat for about 5 minutes or until they begin to become translucent. Add the sugar and cinnamon and cook until the sugar has melted and just begins to caramelize.

- Spread the filling evenly over four crepes, and sprinkle with the cheese. Roll up the crepes and place in the oven, seam side down, for 5 minutes or until the cheese has melted.

Serves 4

Index

Italic numbers indicate illustrations.